BRITISH
WARSHIPS
& AUXILIARIES

NICK NEWNS   **RMAS ADEPT leads HMS OCEAN out of Devonport.**

THE ROYAL NAVY

In Royal Naval circles 2005 will be remembered for two things - the International Fleet Review in the Solent, the spectacular centrepiece of the Trafalgar 200 celebrations and the seemingly endless stream of Royal Navy warships entering UK naval ports for the last time under the White Ensign.

The fleet gathering in the Solent in June was, on the surface, a tremendous PR success - massive crowds and glorious weather (mostly) turned the whole event into something quite memorable. But how many people returned home under the impression that all must be well with the RN - just look at how many ships were in the Solent!

When you have salt water running through your veins it is sometimes difficult to be objective when you see good ships withdrawn from service, apparently for no reason other than economic pressures. Emotions do take over and you tend to enter a downward spiral of doom and gloom, unable to see the light at the end of the tunnel. One can become very pessimistic about the future - I myself am frequently guilty of this!

It cannot be argued that the RN had to evolve to meet the demands of the post Cold War era. For decades its primary purpose had been the protection of the North Atlantic sea lanes from the massive threat posed by the Soviet submarine fleet. With the collapse of the Soviet Union, that threat has almost become a thing of the past and with it, the RN's focus on Anti-submarine warfare had to change. The threat of a super-power versus super-power conflict had receded and ministers, quick as ever to find a money saving opportunity, rightly said that the size and structure of the RN, at that time, needed to be reviewed - the so called "peace dividend" would see force levels reduced to those more in keeping with a peacetime role.

This reshaping of the RN has now been taking place for over 10 years - and the pessimism begins to creep in as force levels continue to drop below those necessary to maintain an effective peacetime fighting force - let alone a force preparing to fight a war one day. Despite the protestations of the RN's professional heads the cuts continued - and the argument of "reshaping" the RN to meet the demands of the current world situation started to wear thin.

In recent years the RN has been actively involved in combat operations in the Adriatic, off Afghanistan, Iraq and West Africa. Never in recent years have so many UK troops been involved in so many combat operations as they are today. UK armed forces are actively engaged in the ongoing War on Terror - yet still the RN is suffering cutbacks. To add insult to injury, warships are being put into reduced support status - laid up alongside with minimal maintenance, in order to save £310 million - the argument being that the money should be concentrated on the "real" frontline services of the Army and RAF operating in Iraq and Afghanistan.

The RN still suffers from the "over the horizon" syndrome - out of sight out of mind. Far from sailing around the world, spending time in exotic destinations the RN has been at the forefront of many operations around the world. RN warships continue to opertate in support of anti-terrorist operations, despite the demise in 2005 of the Northern Ireland Patrol Squadron. RN warships have been the first to appear off foreign shores when emergency evacuations of nationals are required - Albania, Sierra Leone, Liberia, Lebanon, Timor all spring to mind. RN warships have been a detterent in potential world flashpoints - menacingly sitting offshore - their mere presence preventing potential conflict. RN warships have often been the first on the scene in times of world disaster - be it earthquake, tsunami or hurricane. Following the damage in the wake of Hurricane Katrina the majority of the initial response came from the sea. In the Caribbean RN warships have intercepted ton after ton of illegal drugs with a street value of hundreds of millions of pounds but the force level will still be significantly reduced in 2006.

Whilst the World order might have changed, geography certainly has not. The government consistently fail to hoist onboard the fact that we were in the past, are now and will probably remain in the furture, an island nation. Continuing talk of reshaping and restructuring has over the past eight years steadily stripped the RN of many of its essential assets with little or no new tonnage replacing it.

To many the RN is, in today's world, somewhat of a luxury. It is seen as a means of getting the "real" fighting forces delivered to a war zone - becoming in effect a glorified ferry service. It might well have had to change direction. It might well have had to adapt to new roles as forces become more rapidly deployable. It is still true to say, however, that 95% of the equipment logistics chain supporting the Iraq operations was moved by sea.

But to dismiss the RN of today as a luxury, or worse, an irrelavence, is to do it a grave disservice. The RN has been cut back to the bone - commitments have been cut and any increase in the current tempo of operations will place a tremendous strain on the precious few operational ships.

So, as the high profile events of 2005 recede in the memory, what of the future? Many of the re-equipment programmes, which for so long have been marred by cost over-runs and delays, are beginning to bear fruit. The new MoD team appear to be attacking the problems of infrastructure and industrial capacity and future programmes appear to be progressing.

As the RN enters the second half of the first decade of the new millenium, it could be on the brink of rising "phoenix-like" from the ashes as it strives to shake off the wreckless cuts of the past.

What should emerge over the next few years is a modern versatile force - able to react to the requirements of government, wherever, and whenever needed. However, too many would seem to be still just "a twinkle in the eye" with review after review taking place, but little inclination to commit hard cash or to begin metal bashing.

Submarine Fleet

The submarine fleet is ageing rapidly and it is unlikely that the Astute class programme will be able to keep up with demand for replacement hulls. Already the

1997 Strategic Defence Review figure of 10 fleet submarines has been cutback to just eight. By the end of 2006 there will only be two S class boats left in service (SUPERB and SCEPTRE) operating alongside seven T class. With only three Astute class presently on order, and the first of these (ASTUTE) not expected to enter service until 2008, it is likely that SSN numbers will dip below eight. There has long been talk of a second batch of Astutes, indeed it was thought that the future SSN fleet would comprise solely of Astutes, but without new orders in the very near future, there is going to be a delivery gap which will seriously erode the RNs ability to deploy an adequate SSN force.

The four submarine Trident class vessels are expected to serve until 2020 and are presently cycling through a refit programme at Devonport. The government have announced that a decision on a replacement for Trident will be made during this parliamentary term, but it is not known whether this will be a submarine launched Ballistic Missile System, a smaller, shorter range nuclear armed cruise missile system, or as championed by some, a return to long range bombers and air launched cruise missiles. Public opinion is likely to play a large part in this debate - Trident was a massively expensive system to acquire and operate - in today's climate are the public going to want to see such sums spent on what is seen largely as a product of the cold war? A recent MORI poll commissioned by Greenpeace suggests that the majority of people (54%) are against replacing Trident (however, given the wording of the question it is not surprising - *The total cost of replacing 'Trident' missiles, submarines and base facilities is likely to be around £25 billion. This is the equivalent of building around 1,000 new schools at current prices.On balance, do you think the UK should replace its nuclear weapons, or not?*)

The infra structure to support nuclear submarine operations is in place but there is growing public concern over nuclear activities - the UKs refitting facilities at Devonport are under constant fire for being too close to the centre of a population mass. Will such opinion hold sway over any future decisions? It's hard to say - but the nuclear-powered submarine is central to RN operations. The First Sea Lord is certain that the only way he could guarantee to take out a major surface combatant was with a nuclear-powered submarine.

Aircraft Carriers

2005 saw the start of the exit from service of the Invincible class aircraft carriers. These small carriers have served the nation well for over twenty years, but again they were designed during the cold war as an anti-submarine vessel. Throughout their lives the three ships have been continuously upgraded and now operate as a Strike Carrier - deploying to where they are needed with a tailored air group embarked, structured to support the specific mission. INVINCIBLE was placed at extended readiness in 2005 and is scheduled to decommission in 2010. ILLUSTRIOUS and ARK ROYAL will alternate as the active fleet carrier for the immediate future, one ship always being available for operations.

The future of RN fixed wing aviation is vested in the Future Aircraft Carrier (CVF) and the Joint Strike Fighter (JSF). An expensive and ambitious project, the government is taking its time in committing cash to the venture. Having been stung by big budget procurement projects in the past, the MoD are determined to have a concrete package of schedules, costs and designs before proceeding to Main Gate. The truth of the matter may be that there are too many balls in the air and the project has just become too complex.

At the eleventh hour the French announced that CVF may be a solution to their requirement for a second carrier. Although the financial savings to be gained by building three rather than two ships is clear - MoD are determined that French involvement must not delay the UK programme. It is hard to see how delays can be avoided as the French want a conventional carrier and the RN carriers are to be optimised for VSTOL operations.

Could it be that French involvement will finally get the UK MoD to commit to the conventional JSF. The MoDs original order was for the vertical take-off and landing variant of the aircraft. The JSF programme has been fraught with difficulties, particularly regarding weight issues with the UKs preferred variant. The MoD still say they have yet to make the decision on which type will be procured - French involvement might force them down the conventional route to save on differences in carrier design.

Amphibious Fleet

For many years the RN's amphibious capability was run down - the old commando carriers BULWARK, ALBION and HERMES were paid off without replacement and the core of the fleet were the ageing FEARLESS and INTREPID and the equally old LSLs of the RFA.

Today, sealift and the ability to project power from the sea to the shore has seen a rennaissance in Amphibious warfare and the RN now has an Amphibious fleet the envy of many.

HMS OCEAN has been the cornerstone of the Amphibious fleet since entering service in 1998. In recent years she has been joined by the two new LPDs ALBION and BULWARK giving the fleet three very capable amphibious ships, each with full command and control facilities. These will soon be joined by four new RFAs of the Bay class. Designed as replacements for the elderly LSLs, these four ships are LPDs in all but name, lacking only the command and control facilities. Future RN Amphibious Task groups are going to be able to call on a modern, capable fleet of ships to undertake rapid and effective deployments to trouble spots around the world.

Backing up this fleet are the six Ro-Ro vessels of the Point class operated on behalf of the MoD.

Escort Fleet

Without doubt, the RN fleet of destroyers and frigates must be a cause for concern for the nation. With numbers cut to just 25, the RN is going to have to carry out a delicate balancing act to get the best use out of these few ships without driving them into the ground.

The previous sections have demonstrated the number of potential major ships, or "high value units" scheduled to operate in the future RN. This however, has not been matched by a suitable number of escorts to keep these lightly armed ships safe.

Current planning calls for the acquisition of eight Type 45 destroyers to replace the elderly Type 42 ships. Originally to have been a class of up to 12 vessels, three are under construction, with the first scheduled to be launched in February. Final contract terms are still ongoing for a further three and there is much debate as to whether the final two will be ordered, although, in a written parliamentary answer, Adam Ingram said he "expects the period 2012-15 to see the withdrawal from service of the last three Type 42 destroyers, HMS EDINBURGH, HMS NOTTINGHAM and HMS YORK, and their replacement by three further Type 45 destroyers, the first being HMS DUNCAN".

With the oldest Type 23 frigates now 14 years old and the Type 22s even older, consideration is urgently required for a frigate programme to replace the 17 frigates in service. Studies such as the Medium-sized Vessel Derivative or the Versatile Surface Combattant have emerged in the wake of the cancelled Future Surface Combattant programme, but these are working to an assumed in service date of 2023, maybe 2020 at the earliest, by which time the frigate force is going to be very long in the tooth (over 30 years old for the Type 22s).

If the RN is to operate an Amphibious Task Group and a Carrier Strike Group, potentially in littoral waters, the need for escorts to provide anti-submarine and anti-air cover has to be urgently addressed - without doubt the Type 45 is going to be a quantum leap in air defence capability but can eight ships (maybe only six), with some always under repair or in maintenance, really be enough to provide sufficent vessels for large scale operations?

Minor Warships

In March 2005 it was announced that the three patrol vessels of the Northern Ireland Patrol Squadron were to decommission, eighteen months earlier than previously announced. By October all three were at Portsmouth awaiting disposal. It still seems a strange decision, that in these days of an increased terror threat and an international war on terror, that three vessels, operating on anti-terror patrols cannot be found employment around the UK's coastal waters.

The year also saw a change in the structure of the MCM squadrons. By 2007 it is intended that all of the Hunt class vessels will move to Portsmouth and the Sandown class will move to Faslane.

The innovative leasing deal regarding the three River class patrol vessels has been deemed a success, and as the present five year period of operations draws to an end, contract negotiations to extend the deal were ongoing as we went to press. The success of the programme has seen a similar structure put in place for the operation of the new Falkland Islands Patrol Vessel, CLYDE, presently under construction by the VT Group, to replace both LEEDS CASTLE and DUMBARTON CASTLE.

Networked Enabled Capability (NEC)

Much of the MoDs new doctrine for the armed forces centres around this so called NEC. While the aims are laudable, the pitfalls are many.

The idea of having ships, aircraft, infantry, headquarters, allies, all being able to talk to one another, share intelligence, radar pictures, imagery etc may work well in Hollywood, but the practicalities of making such a complex architecture work appear to me to be a money pit.

At the best of times basic communications at sea are fragile. Working between RN ships is well practiced but once a third party is introduced it becomes more complex - some operate with different equipment, privacy systems, some allies won't be privy to all information. How much bandwidth is required for all the feeds? How many different terminal equipments? How much information will be lost if ships have to revert to secondary working? Satellite comms are fine - how many nations have access to anti-satellite missiles? Not many - but then again one only has to target the ground stations to render a complete network inactive. If the UK is developing this capability alone, how will it fit in with the US or the French system? Will the US share information with us if the French, Germans or Spanish are on the same network?

The whole scenario is fraught with problems and the danger is that if certain aspects cannot be resolved, they will be omitted - the bits that can be made to work will be fielded operationally by those units able to operate it - leaving certain operational elements outside of the loop - given the difficulty in long range maritime communications and the amount of bandwidth required, I fear that the RN element of NEC may be the one to be omitted.

Naval Infrastructure

As we closed for press (November 2005) it was expected that a report into a future Defence Industrial Strategy would be published. Undertaken by the government it is hoped that the report will lay the foundations for the future of, among other things, British naval shipbuilding. For too long now Naval Shipbuilders have been at the mercy of the government, not knowing from year to year whether there would be any new work. The periods of feast to famine have all but destroyed this sector of industry. Large gaps in orders means laying off a skilled workforce and in some cases a total loss of capability - the Astute programme is a case in point, where key skills were diminished, workers laid off and in many cases, those core skills lost to the industry for good.

It is likely that the way ahead will be seen as an alliance or consortium of shipbuilders, sharing the work around the various yards in an effort to sustain constant regular work rather than "Feast or famine."

How this will work in practice remains to be seen. Without doubt, there are a lot of ships to be built - at least there is talk of a lot of ships to be built. Can the RN and RFA run on with older ships whilst industry slowly produce vessels over an extended period, or is it essential that a high volume, short time frame approach is adopted? Whatever the outcome, any alliance will have to prove, consistently, that they can build to time and to cost - money for defence related projects is a scarce resource under this government - once it commits money to a project, industry had better be up to the job of delivering - they have failed miserably in the past.

I started off this introduction by saying that I thought the RN had overcome the worst and was now on the road to recovery. The ground work has been laid, future carriers, Type 45 destroyers, Astute submarines, new amphibious and support vessels for the RFA. The plans are ambitious - but the RN, having made the sacrifices already - is in need of this new capability. All it needs is for the government to place the orders and set the RN on the road to recovery.

Steve Bush
November 2005

SHIPS OF THE ROYAL NAVY
Pennant Numbers

Ship	Pennant Number	Page	Ship	Pennant Number	Page
Aircraft Carriers			LANCASTER	F229	18
			ARGYLL	F231	18
INVINCIBLE	R05	13	IRON DUKE	F234	18
ILLUSTRIOUS	R06	13	MONMOUTH	F235	18
ARK ROYAL	R07	13	MONTROSE	F236	18
			WESTMINSTER	F237	18
Assault Ships			NORTHUMBERLAND	F238	18
			RICHMOND	F239	18
OCEAN	L12	14			
ALBION	L14	15	**Submarines**		
BULWARK	L15	15			
			VANGUARD	S28	10
Destroyers			VICTORIOUS	S29	10
			VIGILANT	S30	10
EXETER	D89	16	VENGEANCE	S31	10
SOUTHAMPTON	D90	16	TURBULENT	S87	11
NOTTINGHAM	D91	16	TIRELESS	S88	11
LIVERPOOL	D92	16	TORBAY	S90	11
MANCHESTER	D95	17	TRENCHANT	S91	11
GLOUCESTER	D96	17	TALENT	S92	11
EDINBURGH	D97	17	TRIUMPH	S93	11
YORK	D98	17	SCEPTRE	S104	12
			SPARTAN	S105	12
Frigates			TRAFALGAR	S107	11
			SOVEREIGN	S108	12
KENT	F78	18	SUPERB	S109	12
PORTLAND	F79	18			
GRAFTON	F80	18			
SUTHERLAND	F81	18			
SOMERSET	F82	18			
ST ALBANS	F83	18			
CUMBERLAND	F85	20			
CAMPBELTOWN	F86	20			
CHATHAM	F87	20			
CORNWALL	F99	20			

Ship	Pennant Number	Page	Ship	Pennant Number	Page
Minehunters			MERSEY	P283	24
			SCIMITAR	P284	25
LEDBURY	M30	21	SABRE	P285	25
CATTISTOCK	M31	21	PUNCHER	P291	26
BROCKLESBY	M33	21	CHARGER	P292	26
MIDDLETON	M34	21	RANGER	P293	26
CHIDDINGFOLD	M37	21	TRUMPETER	P294	26
ATHERSTONE	M38	21			
HURWORTH	M39	21	**Survey Ships & RN**		
QUORN	M41	21	**Manned Auxiliaries**		
WALNEY	M104	22			
PENZANCE	M106	22	GLEANER	H86	31
PEMBROKE	M107	22	ECHO	H87	29
GRIMSBY	M108	22	ENTERPRISE	H88	29
BANGOR	M109	22	ROEBUCK	H130	30
RAMSEY	M110	22	SCOTT	H131	28
BLYTH	M111	22	ENDURANCE	A171	32
SHOREHAM	M112	22			
Patrol Craft					
EXPRESS	P163	26			
EXPLORER	P164	26			
EXAMPLE	P165	26			
EXPLOIT	P167	26			
ARCHER	P264	26			
DUMBARTON CASTLE	P265	23			
BITER	P270	26			
SMITER	P272	26			
PURSUER	P273	26			
TRACKER	P274	26			
RAIDER	P275	26			
BLAZER	P279	26			
DASHER	P280	26			
TYNE	P281	24			
SEVERN	P282	24			

HMS Victorious

VANGUARD CLASS

Ship	Pennant Number	Completion Date	Builder
VANGUARD	S28	1992	VSEL
VICTORIOUS	S29	1994	VSEL
VIGILANT	S30	1997	VSEL
VENGEANCE	S31	1999	VSEL

Displacement 15,000 tons (dived) **Dimensions** 150m x 13m x 12m **Speed** 25 + dived **Armament** 16 - Trident 2 (D5) missiles, 4 Torpedo Tubes **Complement** 132

Notes

After the first successful UK D5 missile firing in May '94 the first operational patrol was carried out in early '95 and a patrol has been constantly maintained ever since. According to a parliamentary answer in 2005 the UK's Trident missiles have been de-targeted since 1994, and the submarine on deterrent patrol is normally at several days notice to fire her missiles. The submarines have two crews each to maintain the maximum period on patrol. VICTORIOUS entered refit in 2005 and is scheduled to return to service in 2008.

HMS Trenchant

TRAFALGAR CLASS

Ship	Pennant Number	Completion Date	Builder
TURBULENT	S87	1984	Vickers
TIRELESS	S88	1985	Vickers
TORBAY	S90	1986	Vickers
TRENCHANT	S91	1989	Vickers
TALENT	S92	1990	Vickers
TRIUMPH	S93	1991	Vickers
TRAFALGAR	S107	1983	Vickers

Displacement 4,500 tons **Dimensions** 85m x 10m x 8m **Speed** 30 + dived **Armament** 5 Torpedo Tubes **Complement** 110.

Notes

Quieter, faster and with greater endurance than the Swiftsure class. Tomahawk Cruise Missiles are fitted in TRIUMPH, TRAFALGAR, TURBULENT and TRENCHANT. It is expected Tomahawk will eventually be fitted in all of these boats by 2007. Decommissioning dates announced by the MoD remain: TRAFALGAR (2008); TURBULENT (2009); TIRELESS (2011); TALENT (2017); TRIUMPH (2019); TORBAY (2021) and TRENCHANT (2023).

HMS Sceptre

SWIFTSURE CLASS

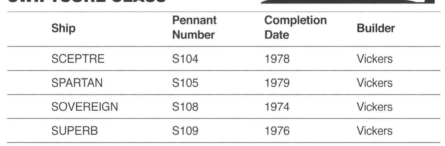

Ship	Pennant Number	Completion Date	Builder
SCEPTRE	S104	1978	Vickers
SPARTAN	S105	1979	Vickers
SOVEREIGN	S108	1974	Vickers
SUPERB	S109	1976	Vickers

Displacement 4,500 tons dived **Dimensions** 83m x 10m x 8m **Speed** 30 knots + dived **Armament** 5 Torpedo Tubes **Complement** 116.

Notes
All are based at Faslane. SPARTAN has been heavily modified to allow the fitting of a dry deck shelter, enabling her to deploy special forces while submerged. Decommissioning dates announced by the MoD are now:- SUPERB (2008) and SCEPTRE (2010). Both SPARTAN and SOVEREIGN are to decommission in 2006. SPLENDID was decommissioned on return from operations off Iraq in 2003 and is laid up at Devonport.

HMS Illustrious

INVINCIBLE CLASS

Ship	Pennant Number	Completion Date	Builder
INVINCIBLE	R05	1979	Vickers
ILLUSTRIOUS	R06	1982	Swan Hunter
ARK ROYAL	R07	1985	Swan Hunter

Displacement 20,700 tons **Dimensions** 206m x 32m x 6.5m **Speed** 28 knots **Armament** 2 - 20mm guns, 3 Phalanx/Goalkeeper **Aircraft** Tailored Air Group (Harrier GR9, Merlin, Sea King, Chinook as required) **Complement** 682 + 366 Fleet Air Arm.

Notes
Recent financial and manpower constraints have seen only one carrier operational. ILLUSTRIOUS assumed the role of fleet flagship in June 2005. ARK ROYAL is the standby carrier, currently at Rosyth preparing for a refit. INVINCIBLE decommissioned in July 2005 and was placed at Extended Readiness at Portsmouth until 2010 when she is likely to be put up for disposal. All can assume the amphibious LPH role. Vessels are now roled as Strike Carriers rather than ASW vessels and as such deploy with a Tailored Air Group to meet the specific operational needs of the deployment.

HMS Ocean

LANDING PLATFORM HELICOPTER (LPH)

Ship	Pennant Number	Completion Date	Builder
OCEAN	L12	1998	Kvaerner

Displacement 21,578 tonnes **Dimensions** 208m x 34m x 6.6m **Speed** 17 knots **Armament** 3 x Phalanx, 6 x 30mm BMARC guns **Complement** Ship 284, Squadrons 180, Embarked force 800.

Notes

Can carry 12 Sea King and 6 Lynx helicopters. Frequently employed as the flagship of the UK Amphibious Ready Group. RAF Chinook helicopters are normally carried as an integral part of the ship's air group, but they are unable to be stowed below decks. During a docking period at the end of 2002 she was modified with two 50m blisters attached to the hull at the waterline below the after chine to improve safety margins while deploying LCVPs from the after davits. The large crane aft of the island (formerly fitted to the diving vessel HMS CHALLENGER), which had been missing throughout 2004, was reinstalled in 2005. Vessel is somewhat constrained by her slow speed.

14

HMS Bulwark

LPD
ALBION CLASS

Ship	Pennant Number	Completion Date	Builder
ALBION	L14	2003	BAE Systems
BULWARK	L15	2004	BAE Systems

Displacement 18,500 tons, 21,500 tons (flooded) **Dimensions** 176m x 25.6m x 6.1m
Speed 18 knots **Armament** 2 x CIWS, 2 x 20mm guns (single) **Complement** 325
Military Lift 303 troops, with an overload capacity of a further 405.

Notes
ALBION commissioned in June 2003, but was at reduced readiness in 2005 undergoing a
capablility upgrade at Devonport. BULWARK was handed over in July 2004 and became
operational in 2005. Vehicle deck capacity for up to six Challenger 2 tanks or around 30
armoured all-terrain tracked vehicles. Floodable well dock, with the capacity to take four utility landing craft. Four smaller landing craft on davits, each capable of carrying 35 troops
each. Two-spot flight deck able to take medium support helicopters and stow a third. The
Flight Deck is capable of taking the Chinook. These vessels do not have a hangar but have
equipment needed to support aircraft operations. Have diesel/electric propulsion.

HMS Southampton

DESTROYERS
SHEFFIELD CLASS
(Type 42) Batch 2

Ship	Pennant Number	Completion Date	Builder
EXETER	D89	1980	Swan Hunter
SOUTHAMPTON	D90	1981	Vosper T.
NOTTINGHAM	D91	1982	Vosper T.
LIVERPOOL	D92	1982	C. Laird

Displacement 3,660 tons **Dimensions** 125m x 15m x 7m **Speed** 29 knots **Armament** 1 - 4.5-inch gun, 4 - 20mm guns, Sea Dart Missile System: 2 - Phalanx, Lynx Helicopter, 6 Torpedo Tubes **Complement** 266.

Notes

Following her 2002 grounding off Australia, NOTTINGHAM was returned to service in 2004 after a £26 million repair at FSL Portsmouth. GLASGOW, NEWCASTLE and CARDIFF paid off in 2005 and are at Portsmouth awaiting disposal. As at June 2005 the following decommissioning dates announced by the MoD remain: LIVERPOOL (2009); EXETER (2009); SOUTHAMPTON (2010) and NOTTINGHAM (2012).

SHEFFIELD CLASS
(Type 42) Batch 3

Ship	Pennant Number	Completion Date	Builder
MANCHESTER	D95	1983	Vickers
GLOUCESTER	D96	1984	Vosper T.
EDINBURGH	D97	1985	C. Laird
YORK	D98	1984	Swan Hunter

Displacement 4,775 tons **Dimensions** 132m x 15m x 7m **Speed** 30 knots + **Armament** 1- 4.5-inch gun, 2 - Phalanx, 2 - 20mm guns, Sea Dart missile system, Lynx Helicopter, 6 Torpedo Tubes **Complement** 269.

Notes
Stretched versions of earlier ships of this class. Designed to provide area defence of a task force. Deck edge stiffening fitted to counter increased hull stress. EDINBURGH and YORK (only) fitted with 4.5-inch Mod 1 gun. In June 2005 the MoD confirmed the following decommissioning dates: MANCHESTER & GLOUCESTER (2011), YORK (2012) & EDINBURGH (2013).

FRIGATES

DUKE CLASS (Type 23)

Ship	Pennant Number	Completion Date	Builder
KENT	F78	2000	Yarrow
PORTLAND	F79	2000	Yarrow
GRAFTON	F80	1996	Yarrow
SUTHERLAND	F81	1997	Yarrow
SOMERSET	F82	1996	Yarrow
ST ALBANS	F83	2001	Yarrow
LANCASTER*	F229	1991	Yarrow
ARGYLL	F231	1991	Yarrow
IRON DUKE*	F234	1992	Yarrow
MONMOUTH*	F235	1993	Yarrow
MONTROSE*	F236	1993	Yarrow
WESTMINSTER	F237	1993	Swan Hunter
NORTHUMBERLAND*	F238	1994	Swan Hunter
RICHMOND	F239	1994	Swan Hunter

Displacement 3,500 tons **Dimensions** 133m x 15m x 5m **Speed** 28 knots **Armament** Harpoon & Seawolf missile systems: 1 - 4.5-inch gun, 2 - single 30mm guns, 4 - 2 twin, magazine launched, Torpedo Tubes, Lynx or Merlin helicopter **Complement** 173.

Notes
The ships incorporate 'Stealth' technology to minimise magnetic, radar, acoustic and infra-red signatures. Gas turbine and diesel electric propulsion. Those ships marked * have been fitted with the Mk 8 Mod 1 4.5-inch gun. The rest of class to be fitted by 2011. Type 2087 Sonar is to be fitted in 12 of the remaining 13 of the class.
NORFOLK and MARLBOROUGH paid off in 2005 as a result of the July 2004 defence cuts with GRAFTON to follow in 2006. All three ships have been sold to Chile in a £135 million deal. All three will be in Chilean service by 2008, replacing three elderly Leander class frigates.

HMS Iron Duke

HMS Northumberland (note new 2087 sonar body in stern)

HMS Chatham

BROADSWORD CLASS
(Type 22) Batch 3

Ship	Pennant Number	Completion Date	Builder
CUMBERLAND	F85	1988	Yarrow
CAMPBELTOWN	F86	1988	C. Laird
CHATHAM	F87	1989	Swan Hunter
CORNWALL	F99	1987	Yarrow

Displacement 4,200 tons **Dimensions** 147m x 15m x 7m **Speed** 30 knots **Armament** 1 - 4.5-inch gun, 1 - Goalkeeper, 8 - Harpoon, 2 - Seawolf, 2 - 20mm guns, 6 Torpedo Tubes, 2 Lynx or 1 Sea King Helicopter **Complement** 259.

Notes
All these ships have an anti-submarine and intelligence gathering capability. All are capable of acting as fleet flagships. CUMBERLAND fitted with Mk8 4.5-inch Mod 1 gun in 2001 and the remainder will be fitted by the end of the decade. Of the Batch II Type 22s BRAVE and BOXER were sunk as fleet targets in August 2004. SHEFFIELD was transferred to Chile as ALMIRANTE WILLIAMS. COVENTRY was handed over to Romania as REGELE FERDINAND in 2004 and LONDON followed in 2005 as REGINA MARIA.

HMS Ledbury

MINE COUNTERMEASURES SHIPS (MCMV'S) HUNT CLASS

Ship	Pennant Number	Completion Date	Builder
LEDBURY	M30	1981	Vosper T.
CATTISTOCK	M31	1982	Vosper T.
BROCKLESBY	M33	1983	Vosper T.
MIDDLETON	M34	1984	Yarrow
CHIDDINGFOLD	M37	1984	Vosper T.
ATHERSTONE	M38	1987	Vosper T.
HURWORTH	M39	1985	Vosper T.
QUORN	M41	1989	Vosper T.

Displacement 625 tonnes **Dimensions** 60m x 10m x 2.2m **Speed** 17 knots **Armament** 1 x 30mm + 2 x 20mm guns **Complement** 42.

Notes

The largest warships ever built of glass reinforced plastic. Their cost (£35m each) has dictated the size of the class. Very sophisticated ships - and lively seaboats! By 2007 all will be based at Portsmouth. Ships are frequently deployed in the Fishery Protection role. Two of the class were sold to Greece in 2000 and 2001. BROCKLESBY, CHIDDING-FOLD, QUORN, HURWORTH and ATHERSTONE are scheduled to decommission in 2020 and LEDBURY in 2023. Under the July 2004 defence cuts COTTESMORE, BRE-CON and DULVERTON (refitted as patrol boats for operations off Northern Ireland) were to be withdrawn from service by April 2007 but all three paid off in 2005 and are at Portsmouth awaiting disposal.

HMS Penzance

SANDOWN CLASS

Ship	Pennant Number	Completion Date	Builder
WALNEY	M104	1992	Vosper T.
PENZANCE	M106	1998	Vosper T.
PEMBROKE	M107	1998	Vosper T.
GRIMSBY	M108	1999	Vosper T.
BANGOR	M109	2000	Vosper T.
RAMSEY	M110	2000	Vosper T.
BLYTH	M111	2001	Vosper T.
SHOREHAM	M112	2001	Vosper T.

Displacement 450 tons **Dimensions** 53m x 10m x 2m **Speed** 13 knots **Armament** 1 - 30mm gun **Complement** 34.

Notes

A class dedicated to a single mine hunting role. Propulsion is by vectored thrust and bow thrusters. By 2007 all will be based at Faslane. CROMER paid off in 2001 and was towed to Dartmouth in 2002 to become a static training hull (renamed HINDUSTAN). BRID-PORT, SANDOWN and INVERNESS all paid off in 2005 as a defence economy and are laid up awaiting disposal at Portsmouth.

HMS Dumbarton Castle

PATROL VESSELS

CASTLE CLASS

Ship	Pennant Number	Completion Date	Builder
DUMBARTON CASTLE	P265	1982	Hall Russell

Displacement 1,450 tons **Dimensions** 81m x 11m x 3m **Speed** 20 knots **Armament** 1 - 30mm gun **Complement** 42

Notes

This ship has a dual role - that of fishery protection and offshore patrols within the limits of UK territorial waters and the Falkland Islands. Unlike the River Class she is able to operate helicopters - including Sea King aircraft. LEEDS CASTLE paid off in August 2005.

A new single Offshore Patrol Vessel (OPV), CLYDE, is to replace the two Castle class ships. CLYDE is scheduled to be launched from Vosper Thornycroft's Portsmouth facility on 20 June 2006 and accepted into service on 31 October. She is expected to deploy to the Falklands for the first time in May 2007. It is envisaged that CLYDE's more modern design will enable her to remain on task in the South Atlantic until 2012.

The 1,850 tonne ship is a River class derivative and will have a crew of 34 and be armed with a single 30mm gun. She will carry out patrol duties around the Falklands and their dependencies, and is able to accommodate a single helicopter up to Merlin size.

HMS Mersey

RIVER CLASS

Ship	Pennant Number	Completion Date	Builder
TYNE	P281	2002	Vosper T.
SEVERN	P282	2003	Vosper T.
MERSEY	P283	2003	Vosper T.

Displacement 1700 tonnes **Dimensions** 80m x 13.5m x 3.8m **Speed** 20+ knots **Armament** 1 x 20mm, 2 x GPMG **Complement** 48

Notes

Ordered on 8 May 2001, the deal is unusual in that the ships are being leased from Vospers (VT) for five years under a £60 million contract. Thereafter the opportunity exists for the lease to be extended, the ships purchased outright or returned to VT. So far the arrangement seems to have been a success with VT meeting their commitment of having the ships available for over 300 days a year.

HMS Sabre

LIFESPAN PATROL VESSELS (LPVs)

Ship	Pennant Number	Completion Date	Builder
SCIMITAR	P284	1988	Halmatic
SABRE	P285	1988	Halmatic

Displacement 18.5 tons **Dimensions** 16m x 4.7m x 1.4m **Speed** 27+ knots
Armament 2 x GPMG **Complement** 4

Notes
Purpose built in 1988 for counter terrorism duties on Lough Neagh, Northern Ireland. Operated in anonimity until withdrawn from service in 2002, following a review of RN operations in the Province. Transferred to Gibraltar in September 2002 to join the Gibraltar Patrol Boat Squadron. On completion of trials they were commissioned on 31 January 2003 and renamed SCIMITAR (ex-GREYFOX) and SABRE (ex-GREY-WOLF). They replaced the P2000 patrol boats TRUMPETER and RANGER.

COASTAL TRAINING CRAFT
P2000 CLASS

Ship	Pennant Number	Completion Date	Builder
EXPRESS	P163	1988	Vosper T.
EXPLORER	P164	1985	Watercraft
EXAMPLE	P165	1985	Watercraft
EXPLOIT	P167	1988	Vosper T.
ARCHER	P264	1985	Watercraft
BITER	P270	1985	Watercraft
SMITER	P272	1986	Watercraft
PURSUER	P273	1988	Vosper T.
TRACKER	P274	1998	Ailsa Troon
RAIDER	P275	1998	Ailsa Troon
BLAZER	P279	1988	Vosper T.
DASHER	P280	1988	Vosper T.
PUNCHER	P291	1988	Vosper T.
CHARGER	P292	1988	Vosper T.
RANGER	P293	1988	Vosper T.
TRUMPETER	P294	1988	Vosper T.

Displacement 43 tonnes **Dimensions** 20m x 6m x 1m **Speed** 20 knots **Armament** 1 x GPMG (Cyprus based vessels) **Complement** 5 (with accommodation for up to 12 under-graduates).

Notes

In service with RN University units (URNU) as training vessels. TRUMPETER and RANGER deployed to Gibraltar in 1991 and armed in 2002. TRUMPETER returned to the UK in 2003 and RANGER followed in 2004. DASHER and PURSUER were transferred to Cyprus at the end of 2002 to form a new Cyprus Squadron to patrol off the Sovereign Base Areas. Remaining vessels are assigned to the following URNUs: ARCHER (Aberdeen); BITER (Manchester); BLAZER (Southampton); CHARGER (Liverpool); TRUMPETER (Bristol); EXAMPLE (Northumbria); EXPLOIT (Birmingham); EXPLORER (Yorkshire); EXPRESS (Wales); PUNCHER (London); RANGER (Sussex); RAIDER (Cambridge); SMITER (Glasgow); TRACKER (Oxford).

P 164

P 164

HMS Explorer

P165

P 165

HMS Example

HMS Scott

SURVEY SHIPS

Ship	Pennant Number	Completion Date	Builder
SCOTT	H 131	1997	Appledore

Displacement 13,300 tonnes **Dimensions** 131.5m x 21.5m x 9m **Speed** 17 knots **Complement** 63

Notes

SCOTT carries a mixture of the latest UK and US survey equipment. The sonar system is US supplied. She operates a three watch system whereby the vessel is run by 42 of her ships company of 63 - with the remainder on leave. Each crew member works 75 days in the ship before having 30 days off, allowing her to spend more than 300 days at sea in a year. These manpower reductions over previous survey ships have been possible because of the extensive use of commercial lean manning methods including unmanned machinery spaces, fixed fire fighting systems and extensive machinery and safety surveillance technology.

HMS Enterprise

ECHO CLASS

Ship	Pennant Number	Completion Date	Builder
ECHO	H 87	2002	Appledore
ENTERPRISE	H 88	2003	Appledore

Displacement 3,470 tonnes **Dimensions** 90m x 16.8m x 5.5.m **Speed** 15 knots **Armament** 1 x 20mm **Complement** 46 (with accommodation for 81)

Notes

In June 2000, a £130 million order was placed with prime contractor Vosper Thornycroft to build and maintain, over a 25 year period, these two new Survey Vessels Hydrographic Oceanographic (SVHO). Both vessels were built by sub-contractor Appledore Shipbuilding Limited. They have a secondary role as mine countermeasures flag ships. ECHO entered service in 2003 and ENTERPRISE followed in 2004. They will be operationally available for 330 days a year. Utilizing a diesel electric propulsion system, they have three main generators. They are the first RN ships to be fitted with Azimuth pod thrusters in place of the more normal shaft and propellor. Each ship carries a named survey launch, PATHFINDER (ECHO) and PIONEER (ENTERPRISE).

HMS Roebuck

COASTAL SURVEY VESSEL

Ship	Pennant Number	Completion Date	Builder
ROEBUCK	H130	1986	Brooke Marine

Displacement 1500 tonnes **Dimensions** 64m x 13m x 4m **Speed** 15 knots
Armament 1 x 20mm; Mk 44 Mini-guns **Complement** 51.

Notes

Able to operate for long periods away from shore support, this ship and the other vessels of the Hydrographic Fleet collect the data that is required to produce the Admiralty Charts and publications which are sold to mariners worldwide. Fitted with the latest fixing aids and sector scanning sonar. Emerged from a refit at Devonport in 2005 which will allow the ship to serve until 2014. Upgrades have included a new armament to complement the emerging frontline operational role for the survey squadron.

• MICHAEL NITZ

HMS Gleaner

INSHORE SURVEY VESSEL

Ship	Pennant Number	Completion Date	Builder
GLEANER	H86	1983	Emsworth

Displacement 22 tons **Dimensions** 14.8m x 4.7m x 1.3m **Speed** 14 knots
Complement 5.

Notes
Small inshore survey craft used for the collection of data from the shallowest inshore
waters. Will remain in service until at least 2007.

HMS Endurance

ICE PATROL SHIP

Ship	Pennant Number	Completion Date	Builder
ENDURANCE	A171	1990	Ulstein-Hatlo

Displacement 5,129 tons **Dimensions** 91m x 17.9m x 6.5m **Speed** 14.9 knots
Armament Small arms **Aircraft** 2 Lynx **Complement** 116

Notes
Chartered for only 7 months in late 1991 to replace the older vessel of the same name.
Originally M/V POLAR CIRCLE, renamed HMS POLAR CIRCLE (A176) and then purchased by MOD(N) and renamed again in October 1992 to current name. Spends 4-6 months each year in the South Atlantic supporting the British Antarctic Survey. Will remain in service until at least 2015.

Griffon 2000 TDX (M) C23

ROYAL MARINE CRAFT

4 GRIFFON 2000 TDX (M) LCAC

Pennants C21 - C24 **G.R.T.** 6.8 tons **Dimensions** 12m x 5m **Speed** 33 knots **Armament** 1 x GPMG **Complement** 2

Notes
Ordered in April 1993, these four lightly armoured Landing Craft Air Cushion (LCAC) are operated by 539 Assault Squadron. Used extensively during the Iraq War to patrol the marshlands and waterways around Basra. They have the capacity to lift 12 fully equipped troops or 2 x 1000kg pallets of stores and are capable of deployment in C-130 Hercules transport aircraft. It is expected that the current fleet of hovercraft will be replaced in around 2007.

SPECIALIST CRAFT

In addition to the familiar Rigid Raiding Craft and Rigid Inflatable Boats the Royal Marines also operate a range of specialist craft for more covert and special operations which can deploy from both ships and submarines. Air transportable Fast Insertion Craft (FIC) with a speed of 55 knots are known to be in service as are advanced wave piercing designs.
Swimmer Delivery Vehicles (SDV), in reality miniature submarines, which can be deployed from dry deck shelters on larger submarines, are also a part of the UK Special Forces inventory.

10 LCU Mk10

Pennants L1001 - L1010 **G.R.T.** 240 tons FL **Dimensions** 29.8m x 7.4m x 1.7m **Speed** 8.5 knots **Complement** 7.

Notes

Ro-Ro style landing craft designed to operate from the Albion class LPDs. Ordered in 1998 from Ailsa Troon. The first two were delivered in 1999. The remainder were built by BAE Systems at Govan. Capable of lifting one Main Battle Tank or four lighter vehicles. Capacity for 120 troops. Several older LCU Mk9s remain in service and saw service in Kuwait during the recent Iraq War.

23 LCVP Mk5

Pennants 9473, 9673-9692, 9707, 9708 **G.R.T.** 25 tons FL **Dimensions** 15m x 4m x 1.5m **Speed** 20 knots **Complement** 3.

Notes

First one ordered in 1995 from Vosper Thornycroft and handed over in 1996. A further four were delivered in December 1996 to operate from OCEAN, with two more for training at RM Poole ordered in 1998. A further 16 were ordered from Babcock in 2001. The Mk 5 can lift 8 tonnes of stores or a mix of 2 tonnes and 35 troops. These vessels have a greater range, lift and speed than the Mk 4s which they are gradually replacing.

SHIPS FOR THE FUTURE FLEET...

ASTUTE

Ordered in 1997, the Astute class submarines were intended, initially, to replace the S class in RN service. The initial history of the programme was one of overspend and delays, leading in 2003 to a restructuring of the entire contract.
The programme now appears to be back on track with key milestones being achieved in order to deliver the first vessel, ASTUTE in August 2008. The other two submarines in the current order are AMBUSH and ARTFUL. It has long been anticipated that a second batch would be ordered but to date this has still not happened.
A future submarine fleet of eight boats is likely to be further reduced if orders for the second batch are not forthcoming in the immediate future.

TYPE 45

The Type 45 Air Defence Destroyers are intended to replace the elderly Type 42s presently in service.
Initially announced as a class of "up to" 12 ships, this was reduced in 2004 to just eight. Three ships, DARING, DIAMOND and DAUNTLESS are on firm order and under construction by BAE SYSTEMS on the Clyde and the VT Group at Portsmouth. A second batch of three, DEFENDER, DRAGON and DUNCAN have been announced and contract negotiations are still ongoing. Although the shipbuilders are keen to get confirmation of hulls 7 and 8 recent talk in government circles has once again been of a class of "up to eight" vessels. The Defence Secretary has spoken of his desire to see all eight ships built - but added the caveat that it wouldn't be "at any price"
The first of class, DARING, is scheduled to be launched from Scotstoun on 1 Febrary 2006.

FUTURE CARRIER PROGRAMME (CVF)

The latest announcement from the Government was that Main Gate investment for this project has slipped even further. A Main Gate decision was expected in December 2005, but this has been put back to April/May 2006. A decision from the French government, regarding a third carrier for service with the French Navy, was still awaited as we went to press in November 2005. The MoD and Industry have admitted, for the first time, that an in service date of 2012 for the first carrier is unlikely to be achieved. Keen to avoid the slippages and massive increases in budget of recent projects, the MoD wants to be sure that the design, costs and production schedule are set in concrete before committing themselves to ordering these ships. A new predicted in service date will not be announced until contracts are signed and an order placed.

MILITARY AFLOAT REACH AND SUSTAINABILITY (MARS)

The future re-equipment of the RFA rests with this programme which could see between 8 and 15 vessels built. It is hoped that a potential project integrator (in effect a hybrid of Prime contractor and project manager) will be chosen in 2006 with a main investment decision made in 2008 with ships entering service between 2010 and 2020.
The project could be met by up to three classes of vessel - Tankers; Fleet supply vessels optimised to support the Future Carrier and Sea based logistics ships.

JOINT CASUALTY TREATMENT SHIP (JCTS)

Although the JCTS project team was still in place in 2005, with the extension in service of RFA ARGUS to 2020 it is to all intents and purposes a project in abeyance. With the announcement of the MARS project it is quite possible that the JCTS requirement will be absorbed into the larger programme.

THE ROYAL FLEET AUXILIARY

The RFA is a civilian manned service; all the RFA crews follow the same training and achieve the same commercial qualifications as their Merchant Navy counterparts. The ships come under Lloyd's classification and categorisation. This makes sense as the core task for the ships are the loading and discharging of stores, containers as well as the transport of personnel (troops), their equipment and vehicles. Not to mention the requirement to load and discharge diesel, aviation spirit and bulk oils.

Most RFA's have flight decks and hangars for Sea King, Lynx and Merlin helicopters and these facilities have seen ships of the RFA take on a more important operational role as their extensive flight facilities are used to augment operational forces - the Wave class deploy to the Caribbean with helicopters to assist in the counter drug operations; the Fort class can deploy with Sea King or Merlin to provide additional anti-submarine or maritime strike capability - whilst still carrying over 12,000 tons of fuel and 6000 tons of stores. RFA ARGUS has a peace time role, training pilots in deck landings, and can hangar 6 Sea King helicopters. She is also designated as a Primary Casualty Handling Facility with a 100 bed hospital, 3 operating theatres, and is capable of transporting 12 Harrier aircraft if required, not to mention over 3000 tons of marine diesel and 1100 tons of aviation fuel. RFA DILIGENCE has a full dynamic positioning capability to bring her precisely alongside any other vessel (including submarines) to provide ship repair workshops, electrical power, fuel, steam and air. In 2005 she acted as an HQ ship for the fledgling Iraqi Navy, as well as supporting the submarine SPARTAN in both the Indian Ocean and South American waters

The RFA also provides ships for land forces. The Sir Galahad class has been designed to carry over 300 troops, tanks and other vehicles. They have the capability to ground on a beach and discharge the troops and equipment directly to the shore. This class is being replaced by the new highly sophisticated Bay Class Logistic Ships, which have their own internal dock. The final ships of the class, CARDIGAN BAY and LYME BAY were launched in 2005. MOUNTS BAY and LARGS BAY are already afloat, and are being fitted out before coming into service.

An area for concern is the number of single-hulled tankers in service, four Leaf class, three Rover and two Forts. These ageing tankers will be outlawed by 2010 (although there is an exemption for government owned vessels) so the large multi class MARS programme is essential for the future of the RFA.

To this day the RFA has a strong permanent presence in the Persian Gulf and the Atlantic, as well as supporting the Royal Navy on worldwide deployments.

Today's RFA is a world leader in versatile integrated afloat support, not limited to bombs beans and bullets, but a constantly evolving and moving organisation As a busy and effective force multiplier, the RFA is capable of operating alone or as an integral part of a large multi-national task group.

SHIPS OF THE ROYAL FLEET AUXILIARY
Pennant Numbers

Ship	Pennant Number	Ship	Pennant Number	Ship	Pennant Number
BRAMBLELEAF	A81	BLACK ROVER	A273	SIR GALAHAD	L3005
BAYLEAF	A109	FORT ROSALIE	A385	LARGS BAY	L3006
ORANGELEAF	A110	FORT AUSTIN	A386	LYME BAY	L3007
OAKLEAF	A111	FORT VICTORIA	A387	MOUNTS BAY	L3008
DILIGENCE	A132	FORT GEORGE	A388	CARDIGAN BAY	L3009
ARGUS	A135	WAVE KNIGHT	A389	SIR TRISTRAM	L3505
GREY ROVER	A269	WAVE RULER	A390		
GOLD ROVER	A271	SIR BEDIVERE	L3004		

KEEP UP TO DATE THROUGHOUT THE YEAR

Warship World is published six times a year (Jan, Mar, May, Jul, Sep, Nov) and gives you all the information necessary to keep this book updated throughout the year. Now in full colour.

RFA Wave Ruler

FLEET TANKERS
WAVE CLASS

Ship	Pennant Number	Completion Date	Builder
WAVE KNIGHT	A 389	2002	BAE SYSTEMS
WAVE RULER	A 390	2002	BAE SYSTEMS

Displacement 31,500 tons (Full Load) **Dimensions** 196 x 27 x 10m **Speed** 18 knots
Armament 2 x Vulcan Phalanx (fitted for but not with), 2 x 30mm **Aircraft** 1 Merlin
Complement 80 (plus 22 Fleet Air Arm)

Notes

WAVE KNIGHT was accepted into service in March 2003. WAVE RULER followed in
April 2003. These 31,500-tonne ships are diesel-electric powered, with three refuel-
ing rigs, and aviation facilities to operate Merlin helicopters. They have a cargo
capacity of 16,900 tonnes (Fuel) and 915 tonnes (Dry Stores).

RFA Oakleaf

SUPPORT TANKERS

Ship	Pennant Number	Completion Date	Builder
OAKLEAF	A111	1981	Uddevalla

Displacement 49,310 tons **Dimensions** 173.7m x 32.2m x 11.2m **Speed** 14 knots **Complement** 35.

Notes

At 49,310 tons displacement, she is the largest vessel in RN/RFA service. Her role, along with other support tankers, is to provide the fuel vital to enable the Navy's warships to operate far from their UK bases. Originally acquired on Bareboat charter, the ship was purchased by the MoD in September 2004. Decommissioning date has been brought forward from 2015 to 2010.

RFA Orangeleaf

LEAF CLASS

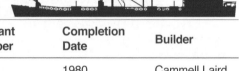

Ship	Pennant Number	Completion Date	Builder
BRAMBLELEAF	A81	1980	Cammell Laird
BAYLEAF	A109	1982	Cammell Laird
ORANGELEAF	A110	1982	Cammell Laird

Displacement 37,747 tons **Dimensions** 170m x 26m x 12m **Speed** 14.5 knots **Complement** 60.

Notes

All are ex-merchant ships, originally acquired for employment mainly on freighting duties. All have been modified to enable them to refuel warships at sea. BRAMBLE-LEAF is MoD(N) owned, the remainder on long-term bareboat charter. All are commercial Stat32 class tankers. ORANGELEAF and BRAMBLELEAF are to decommission in 2009 and BAYLEAF in 2010.

The MoD also has the commercial tanker MAERSK RAPIER on permanent charter. She is a multi-tasked tanker which supplies fuel to the naval facilities in the UK, Gibraltar, the Falkland Islands and Souda Bay, Crete. She is also chartered to supply aviation fuel to Cyprus, Ascension Island and the Falkland Islands. The MoD charters the vessel to commercial companies when it is not in use for their own requirements.

RFA Grey Rover

ROVER CLASS

Ship	Pennant Number	Completion Date	Builder
GREY ROVER	A269	1970	Swan Hunter
GOLD ROVER	A271	1974	Swan Hunter
BLACK ROVER	A273	1974	Swan Hunter

Displacement 11,522 tons **Dimensions** 141m x 19m x 7m **Speed** 18 knots **Armament** 2 - 20mm guns **Complement** 49/54

Notes

Small Fleet Tankers designed to supply warships with fresh water, dry cargo and refrigerated provisions, as well as a range of fuels and lubricants. Helicopter deck, but no hangar. Have been employed in recent years mainly as support for HM Ships operating around the Falkland Islands and West Indies, spending up to two years on deployment in these areas. GREY ROVER is to decommission in 2006, followed by GOLD ROVER in 2009 and BLACK ROVER in 2010.

RFA Fort Austin

STORES VESSELS
FORT CLASS I

Ship	Pennant Number	Completion Date	Builder
FORT ROSALIE	A385	1978	Scott Lithgow
FORT AUSTIN	A386	1979	Scott Lithgow

Displacement 23,384 tons **Dimensions** 183m x 24m x 9m **Speed** 20 knots **Complement** 201, (120 RFA, 36 MoD Civilians & 45 Fleet Air Arm).

Notes
Full hangar and maintenance facilities are provided and up to four Sea King helicopters can be carried for both the transfer of stores and anti-submarine protection of a group of ships. Both ships can be armed with 4 - 20mm guns. FORT ROSALIE is to decommission in 2013 and FORT AUSTIN in 2014.

RFA Fort George

REPLENISHMENT SHIPS
FORT CLASS II

Ship	Pennant Number	Completion Date	Builder
FORT VICTORIA	A387	1992	Harland & Wolff
FORT GEORGE	A388	1993	Swan Hunter

Displacement 35,500 tons **Dimensions** 204m x 30m x 9m **Speed** 20 knots **Armament** 4 - 30mm guns, 2 x Phalanx CIWS, Sea Wolf Missile System (Fitted for but not with) **Complement** 100 (RFA), 24 MoD Civilians, 32 RN and up to 122 Fleet Air Arm.

Notes

"One stop" replenishment ships with the widest range of armaments, fuel and spares carried. Can operate up to 5 Sea King/ 3 Merlin Helicopters (more in a ferry role) with full maintenance facilities onboard. Medical facilities were upgraded with a 12 bed surgical capability to give the vessels a limited role as Primary Casualty Receiving Ships. Both are to remain in service until 2019.

LANDING SHIPS (LOGISTIC)
SIR CLASS

Ship	Pennant Number	Completion Date	Builder
SIR BEDIVERE	L3004	1967	Hawthorn
SIR GALAHAD	L3005	1987	Swan Hunter
SIR TRISTRAM	L3505	1967	Hawthorn

Displacement 5,550 tons **Dimensions** 126m x 18m x 4m **Speed** 17 knots **Armament** Can be fitted with 20 or 40mm guns in emergency **Complement** 65, (SIR GALAHAD is larger at 8,451 tons. 140m x 20m **Complement** 58)

Notes
Manned by the RFA but tasked by the Commodore Amphibious Task Group (COMATG), these ships are used for heavy secure transport of stores – embarked by bow and stern doors. Can operate helicopters from both vehicle and flight decks if required and carry 340 troops. SIR TRISTRAM was rebuilt after extensive Falklands War damage. After extensive delays, SIR BEDIVERE completed a Ship Life Extension Programme (SLEP) at Rosyth in 1998. She is now 7,700 tonnes displacement and her dimensions are 137 x 20 x 4 metres. Occasionally used for MCMV support. SIR GERAINT paid off in 2003 and SIR PERCIVALE in 2004. SIR GALAHAD and SIR TRISTRAM are to pay off in 2006. SIR BEDIVERE is likely to continue in service until 2017.

RFA Mounts Bay

LANDING SHIP DOCK (AUXILIARY) BAY CLASS

Ship	Pennant Number	Completion Date	Builder
LARGS BAY	L3006	2005	Swan Hunter
LYME BAY	L3007	2006	Swan Hunter
MOUNTS BAY	L3008	2005	BAE SYSTEMS
CARDIGAN BAY	L3009	2006	BAE SYSTEMS

Displacement 16,190 tonnes **Dimensions** 176.6m x 26.4m x 5.1m **Speed** 18 knots **Armament** Fitted to receive in emergency **Complement** 60

Notes
Scheduled to start entering service in 2004 the ships have been delayed by 2 years. MOUNTS BAY was expected to be handed over in December 2005, with a mid-2006 in service date. The final vessel is now scheduled to be handed over in 2006. In 2002 the vessels were designated LSD(A) to meet NATO designation requirements for a vessel that has an integral dock. The dock is capable of operating LCU 10s and they carry two LCVP Mk5s. They can offload at sea, over the horizon. In addition to their war fighting role they could be well suited to disaster relief and other humanitarian missions.

RFA Diligence

FORWARD REPAIR SHIP

Ship	Pennant Number	Completion Date	Builder
DILIGENCE	A132	1981	Oesundsvarvet

Displacement 10,595 tons **Dimensions** 120m x 12m x 3m **Speed** 15 knots **Armament** 2 - 20mm **Complement** RFA 40, RN Personnel - approx 100.

Notes

Formerly the M/V Stena Inspector purchased (£25m) for service in the South Atlantic. Her deep diving complex was removed and workshops added. When not employed on "battle repair" duties can serve as support vessel for MCMVs and submarines on deployment. Scheduled to decommission in 2006, this date has now been extended to 2014. A probable replacement will be required, the likely earliest date for such being 2014.

AVIATION TRAINING SHIP

Ship	Pennant Number	Completion Date	Builder
ARGUS	A135	1981	Cantieri Navali Breda

Displacement 28,481 tons (full load) **Dimensions** 175m x 30m x 8m **Speed** 18 knots
Armament 4 - 30 mm, 2 - 20 mm **Complement** 254 (inc 137 Fleet Air Arm)
Aircraft 6 Sea King/Merlin, 12 Harriers can be carried in a "ferry role".

Notes

Formerly the M/V CONTENDER BEZANT taken up from trade during the Falklands crisis. Purchased in 1984 (£13 million) for conversion to an 'Aviation Training Ship'. A £50 million re-build was undertaken at Belfast from 1984-87. Undertook rapid conversion in October 1990 to a Primary Casualty Reception Ship for service in the Gulf. These facilities were upgraded and made permanent during 2001. Originally scheduled to decommission in 2008, this date has now been extended to 2020. A replacement for the Aviation Ship and PCRS role is currently under review. A new RFA PCRS is almost certain, but probaly not in a dual role as an Aviation ship and PCRS. If a new purpose-built/adapted ship is not acquired a likely scenario is that other RFAs with deck/hangar facilities will be used for aviation training (as is the case now when ARGUS is unavailable) or the task may be carried out on RN ships' flight decks.

• DANIEL FERRO

MV Hartland Point

STRATEGIC SEALIFT RO-RO VESSELS

Ship	Pennant Number	Completion Date	Builder
HURST POINT		2002	Flensburger
HARTLAND POINT		2002	Harland & Wolff
EDDYSTONE		2002	Flensburger
LONGSTONE		2003	Flensburger
ANVIL POINT		2003	Harland & Wolff
BEACHY HEAD		2003	Flensburger

Displacement 10,000 tonnes, 13,300 tonnes (FL) **Dimensions** 193m x 26m x 6.6m
Speed 18 knots **Complement** 38

Notes
Foreland Shipping Limited (formerly AWSR) built 6 ro-ro vessels at yards in the UK and Germany under a PFI deal which was signed with the MoD on 27 June 2002 and runs until 31 December 2024. The Strategic Sealift Service requires Foreland to supply four vessels to the MoD on a full time basis with the other two vessels being available only to cover a limited number of pre-determined situations. The two vessels not employed by the MoD, BEACHY HEAD and LONGSTONE, are on charter to Transfennica, a Finnish subsidiary of the Spliethoff Group. The company itself and its six ships are all named after English light-houses. The ships come under the operational umbrella of Defence Supply Chain Operation and Movements (DSCOM), part of the Defence Logistics Organisation.

HMS OCEAN

Nick Newns

HMS NOTTINGHAM

Stuart Miller

Maritime Photographic

HMS ENDURANCE

Nick Newns

A171

Maritime Photographic

HMS HURWORTH

HMS ILLUSTRIOUS

Garry Lakin

RFA MOUNTS BAY

MOUNTS BAY

L3008

Douglas S. Coull

RMAS MENAI and CAREFUL at Falmouth

Dave Fortey

MARINE SERVICES SUPPORT

The Defence Logistic Organisation (DLO) is tasked with Tri-Service provision of Marine Services and is responsible for In and Out-of-Port maritime services in support of Naval Bases, CinC Fleet, The Meteorological Office, QinetiQ (formerly DERA), RAF and Army. Their role is to undertake Mooring and Navigation buoy maintenance, maritime support to the underwater research programme and sea-borne services to the Fleet.

Maritime services at the Kyle of Lochalsh are provided primarily to support the BUTEC Ranges, and secondarily to fulfil Fleet requirements in that area. In the three main ports at Portsmouth, Devonport and Clyde the service is currently delivered under a Government Owned/Commercially Operated (GOCO) contract with SERCo-Denholm Ltd. The vessels being operated on a BARECON (Bareboat charter) basis.

The current provision of marine service support is out for re-tender. The RMAS have been given the opportunity of bidding for a percentage of the work similar to that which they undertake at present. Industry are being allowed to bid for (a) all of the work and (b) all of the work with the RMAS as a partner. Within all solutions both the RMAS and industry are being offered all existing assets and have been encouraged to submit a vessel replacement programme.

For Mooring Maintenance, RMAS NEWTON and services at Kyle of Lochalsh, the service is currently delivered in house by the General Manager RMAS from his HQ at Pembroke Dock.

A 10-year PPP/PFI contract with an effective date of 1 April 2002 was placed with Smit International (Scotland) Ltd to carry out Marine Support to Ranges and Air Crew Training. Since that date Smit have replaced all the MoD craft with a fleet of new and second hand tonnage.

Marine Services vessels can be seen at work in the UK Naval Bases and are easily identified by their black hulls, buff coloured superstructure and by their Flag, which in the case of GM RMAS vessels, is a blue ensign defaced in the fly by a yellow anchor over two wavy lines. The remaining vessels fly the other Government' ensign. Which is a blue ensign defaced in the fly by a yellow anchor.

SHIPS OF
THE MARINE SERVICES
Pennant Numbers

Ship	Pennant Number	Page	Ship	Pennant Number	Page
MELTON	A83	71	ADEPT	A224	60
MENAI	A84	71	BUSTLER	A225	60
MEON	A87	71	CAPABLE	A226	60
TORNADO	A140	74	CAREFUL	A227	60
TORMENTOR	A142	74	FAITHFUL	A228	60
WATERMAN	A146	73	COL. TEMPLER	A229	65
FRANCES	A147	63	DEXTEROUS	A231	60
FLORENCE	A149	63	ADAMANT	A232	70
GENEVIEVE	A150	63	SHEEPDOG	A250	61
KITTY	A170	62	NEWHAVEN	A280	67
LESLEY	A172	62	NUTBOURNE	A281	67
HUSKY	A178	61	NETLEY	A282	67
SALUKI	A182	61	OBAN	A283	68
SALMOOR	A185	75	ORONSAY	A284	68
SALMAID	A187	75	OMAGH	A285	68
BOVISAND	A191	66	PADSTOW	A286	69
CAWSAND	A192	66	IMPULSE	A344	59
HELEN	A198	63	IMPETUS	A345	59
MYRTLE	A199	62	NEWTON	A367	64
SPANIEL	A201	61	WARDEN	A368	77
FORCEFUL	A221	60	OILPRESS	Y21	72
NIMBLE	A222	60	MOORHEN	Y32	76
POWERFUL	A223	60	MOORFOWL	Y33	76

MV Impulse

TUGS

IMPULSE CLASS

Ship	Pennant Number	Completion Date	Builder
IMPULSE	A344	1993	R. Dunston
IMPETUS	A345	1993	R. Dunston

G.R.T. 400 tons approx **Dimensions** 33m x 10m x 4m **Speed** 12 knots **Complement** 5.

Notes
Completed in 1993 specifically to serve as berthing tugs for the Trident Class submarines at Faslane. Both operated under contract by Serco Denholm.

MV Nimble

TWIN UNIT TRACTOR TUGS (TUTT'S)

Ship	Pennant Number	Completion Date	Builder
FORCEFUL	A221	1985	R. Dunston
NIMBLE	A222	1985	R. Dunston
POWERFUL	A223	1985	R. Dunston
ADEPT	A224	1980	R. Dunston
BUSTLER	A225	1981	R. Dunston
CAPABLE	A226	1981	R. Dunston
CAREFUL	A227	1982	R. Dunston
FAITHFUL	A228	1985	R. Dunston
DEXTEROUS	A231	1986	R. Dunston

G.R.T. 375 tons **Dimensions** 39m x 10m x 4m **Speed** 12 knots **Complement** 9.

Notes

The principal harbour tugs in naval service. All operated under contract by Serco Denholm except CAPABLE at Gibraltar which is managed locally.

MV Saluki

DOG CLASS

Ship	Pennant Number	Completion Date	Builder
HUSKY	A178	1969	Appledore
SALUKI	A182	1969	Appledore
SPANIEL	A201	1967	Appledore
SHEEPDOG	A250	1969	Appledore

G.R.T. 152 tons **Dimensions** 29m x 8m x 4m **Speed** 12 knots **Complement** 5.

Notes

General harbour tugs – all completed between 1965 and 1969. COLLIE and CAIRN replaced at Kyle of Lochalsh by civilian vessels under charter to MoD during 2001. SETTER is (2005) on the disposal list and has been replaced for evaluation trials by the tug MT ATLAS which has been bareboat chartered by SERCo/Denholm at Portsmouth. SALUKI operates at Devonport, SHEEPDOG was scheduled to be withdrawn in 2005 but remains in service at Portsmouth. SPANIEL and HUSKY operate on the Clyde.

MV Myrtle

TRITON CLASS

Ship	Pennant Number	Completion Date	Builder
KITTY	A170	1972	R. Dunston
LESLEY	A172	1973	R. Dunston
MYRTLE	A199	1973	R. Dunston

G.R.T. 89 tons **Speed** 8 knots **Complement** 4.

Notes

Known as Water Tractors these craft are used for basin moves and towage of light barges. Operated by Serco Denholm Ltd. KITTY was proposed to be withdrawn from operations in 2003 but remains in service at Portsmouth. LESLEY and MYRTLE operate at Devonport.

MV Frances

FELICITY CLASS

Ship	Pennant Number	Completion Date	Builder
FLORENCE	A149	1980	R. Dunston
FRANCES	A147	1980	R. Dunston
GENEVIEVE	A150	1980	R. Dunston
HELEN	A198	1974	R. Dunston

G.R.T. 80 tons **Speed** 10 knots **Complement** 4.

Notes
Water Tractors used for the movement of small barges and equipment. All are operated by Serco Denholm. Two sister vessels (GEORGINA and GWENDOLINE) sold to Serco Denholm in 1996 for service in H M Naval bases. FLORENCE and FRANCES operate at Devonport, GENEVIEVE and HELEN at Portsmouth.

RMAS Newton

RESEARCH VESSELS

Ship	Pennant Number	Completion Date	Builder
NEWTON	A367	1976	Scotts

G.R.T. 2,779 tons **Dimensions** 99m x 16m x 6m **Speed** 15 knots **Complement** 27

Notes
Primarily used in the support of RN training exercises. Some limited support provided for various trials. Operated by the RMAS. Completed major refit in 2001 to extend life. Is frequently seen with Royal Marine small craft embarked and is used as a training platform.

• DAVE CULLEN

MV Colonel Templer

Ship	Pennant Number	Completion Date	Builder
COLONEL TEMPLER A 229		1966	Hall Russell

Displacement 1,300 tons **Dimensions** 56m x 11m x 5.6 m **Speed** 12 knots
Complement 14

Notes

Built as a stern trawler but converted in 1980 for use by the Defence Evaluation and Research Agency as an acoustic research vessel. A major rebuild was completed after a serious fire gutted the ship in 1990. 12 scientists can be carried. From Nov 2000 operated on the Clyde by Serco Denholm. Used in support of trials and converted in 2001 to support RN diving training.

MV Bovisand

TENDERS
STORM CLASS

Ship	Pennant Number	Completion Date	Builder
BOVISAND	A191	1997	FBM (Cowes)
CAWSAND	A192	1997	FBM (Cowes)

G.R.T 225 tonnes **Dimensions** 23m x 11m x 2m **Speed** 15 knots **Complement** 5

Notes

These craft are used in support of Flag Officer Sea Training (FOST) at Plymouth to transfer staff quickly and comfortably to and from Warships and Auxiliaries within and beyond the Plymouth breakwater in open sea conditions. These are the first vessels of a small waterplane area twin hull (SWATH) design to be ordered by the Ministry of Defence and cost £6.5 million each. Speed restrictions implemented due to wash problems generated by these vessels.

MV Newhaven

NEWHAVEN CLASS

Ship	Pennant Number	Completion Date	Builder
NEWHAVEN	A280	2000	Aluminium SB
NUTBOURNE	A281	2000	Aluminium SB
NETLEY	A282	2001	Aluminium SB

Tonnage 77 tonnes (45 grt) **Dimensions** 18.3m x 6.8m x 1.88m **Speed** 10 knots **Complement** 3 Crew (60 passengers).

Notes
MCA Class IV Passenger Vessels based at Portsmouth as replacements for Fleet tenders. Employed on general passenger duties within the port area.

MV Oronsay

OBAN CLASS

Ship	Pennant Number	Completion Date	Builder
OBAN	A283	2000	McTay
ORONSAY	A284	2000	McTay
OMAGH	A285	2000	McTay

Tonnage 199 tons **Dimensions** 27.7m x 7.30m x 3.75m **Speed** 10 knots **Complement** 5 Crew (60 passengers).

Notes
MCA Class IIA Passenger Vessels which replaced Fleet tenders in 2001. OBAN was transferred to Devonport in 2003 for use in supporting passenger transfers (other than FOST) and duties previously undertaken by LADYBIRD. ORONSAY and OMAGH employed on general passenger duties on the Clyde.

MV Padstow

PADSTOW CLASS

Ship	Pennant Number	Completion Date	Builder
PADSTOW	A286	2000	Aluminium SB

Tonnage 77 tonnes (45 grt) **Dimensions** 18.3m x 6.8m x 1.88m **Speed** 10 knots **Complement** 3 Crew (60 passengers).

Notes
MCA Class VIA Passenger Vessel based at Plymouth. Used on general passenger ferrying duties and in support of FOST staff.

MV Adamant

PERSONNEL FERRY

Ship	Pennant Number	Completion Date	Builder
ADAMANT	A232	1992	FBM (Cowes)

G.R.T 170 tonnes **Dimensions** 30m x 8m x 1m **Speed** 22 knots **Complement** 5

Notes

Twin catamaran hulls based on the commercial Red Jet design (as used by Red Funnel Ferry Co). First water jet propulsion vessel owned by MoD(N). In service as a Clyde personnel ferry - operated by Serco Denholm.

MV Melton

FLEET TENDERS

Ship	Pennant Number	Completion Date	Builder
MELTON	A83	1981	Richard Dunston
MENAI	A84	1981	Richard Dunston
MEON	A87	1982	Richard Dunston

G.R.T. 78 tons **Dimensions** 24m x 6m x 3m **Speed** 10.5 knots **Complement** 4/5.

Notes

The last three survivors of a once numerous class of vessels used as Training Tenders, Passenger Ferries, or Cargo Vessels. MENAI and MEON are operated by Serco Denholm at Falmouth. MELTON is operated by the RMAS at Kyle. Expected to remain in service until the new contract for the Future Provision of Marine Services comes into service, an aspect of which will include a vessel replacement programme.

MV Oilpress

COASTAL OILER

Ship	Pennant Number	Completion Date	Builder
OILPRESS	Y21	1969	Appledore Shipbuilders

G.R.T. 362 tons **Dimensions** 41m x 9m x 3m **Speed** 11 knots **Complement** 5.

Notes
Employed as Harbour and Coastal Oiler. Operated by Serco Denholm on the Clyde.

MV Waterman

WATER CARRIER

Ship	Pennant Number	Completion Date	Builder
WATERMAN	A146	1978	R. Dunston

G.R.T. 263 tons **Dimensions** 40m x 8m x 2m **Speed** 11 knots **Complement** 5.

Notes
Capable of coastal passages, but normally supplies either demineralised or fresh water to the Fleet within port limits. WATERFOWL is owned and operated by Serco Denholm.

MV Tornado

TORPEDO RECOVERY VESSELS (TRV)
TORNADO CLASS

Ship	Pennant Number	Completion Date	Builder
TORNADO	A140	1979	Hall Russell
TORMENTOR	A142	1980	Hall Russell

G.R.T. 560 tons **Dimensions** 47m x 8m x 3m **Speed** 14 knots **Complement** 13.

Notes
All vessels have had suitable rails fitted to enable them to operate as exercise minelayers. Converted in 2002 to support RN diving training (in lieu of Fleet Tenders) in addition to their other roles. Both operate on the Clyde.

RMAS Salmoor

MOORING & SALVAGE VESSELS
SAL CLASS

Ship	Pennant Number	Completion Date	Builder
SALMOOR	A185	1985	Hall Russell
SALMAID	A187	1986	Hall Russell

Displacement 2,200 tonnes **Dimensions** 77m x 15m x 4m **Speed** 15 knots
Complement 19

Notes
Multi-purpose vessels designed to lay and maintain underwater targets, navigation marks and moorings. SALMOOR is based at Greenock and SALMAID at Devonport. Both vessels deployed to the Mediterranean at varying times in 2005 in support of submarine operations and a submarine rescue exercise.

MV Moorfowl

MOOR CLASS

Ship	Pennant Number	Completion Date	Builder
MOORHEN	Y32	1989	McTay Marine
MOORFOWL	Y33	1989	McTay Marine

Displacement 518 tons **Dimensions** 32m x 11m x 2m **Speed** 8 knots **Complement** 10

Notes
Powered mooring lighters for use within sheltered coastal waters. Both operated by the RMAS in support of mooring maintenance. MOORHEN based at Portsmouth and MOORFOWL at Devonport. Both vessels also undertake coastal work.

MV Warden

TRIALS VESSEL

Ship	Pennant Number	Completion Date	Builder
WARDEN	A368	1989	Richards

Displacement 626 tons **Dimensions** 48m x 10m x 4m **Speed** 15 knots **Complement** 11.

Notes

Built as a Range Maintenance Vessel but since, based at Kyle of Lochalsh and operated by the RMAS in support of BUTEC. Her earlier gantry has been removed and bridge structure extended aft. Also operates as a Remotely Operated Vehicle (ROV) platform. A replacement ROV has been installed and set to work to replace the older system.

The RMAS have taken two further trials craft on long term charter to help with the various tasks at the Kyle of Lochalsh. These are the SARA MAATJE VI on charter from Van Stee of Holland and LENIE on charter from Maritime Craft Services of Scotland.

Smit Towy

AIRCREW TRAINING VESSELS

Ship	Comp Date	Builder	Base Port
SMIT DEE	2003	BES Rosyth	Bukie
SMIT DART	2003	BES Rosyth	Plymouth
SMIT DON	2003	BES Rosyth	Blyth
SMIT YARE	2003	FBMA Cebu	Great Yarmouth
SMIT TOWY	2003	FBMA Cebu	Pembroke Dock
SMIT SPEY	2003	FBMA Cebu	Plymouth

G.R.T. 95.86 GRT **Dimensions** 27.6m x 6.6m x 1.5m **Speed** 21 knots **Complement** 6

Notes

The vessels were designed by FBM Babcock Marine and built in their shipyards in Scotland and the Philippines. Operated by SMIT International (Scotland) on behalf of the MoD for training military aircrew in marine survival techniques, helicopter winching drills and general marine support tasks. The design includes an aft docking well for a RIB or for torpedo recovery, a full width stern training platform and clear deck areas for helicopter winching drills. SMIT DART completed as a passenger vessel with larger superstructure. Two similar second-hand vessels, SMIT TAMAR and SMIT CYMYRAN are also employed in the same role. These vessels replaced the former RAF Spitfire class RTTLs in service.

RANGE SAFETY VESSELS

Ship	Comp Date	Builder
SMIT STOUR	2003	Maritime Partners Norway
SMIT ROTHER	2003	Maritime Partners Norway
SMIT ROMNEY	2003	Maritime Partners Norway
SMIT CERNE	2003	Maritime Partners Norway
SMIT FROME	2003	Maritime Partners Norway
SMIT MERRION	2003	Maritime Partners Norway
SMIT PENALLY	2003	Maritime Partners Norway
SMIT WAY	2003	Maritime Partners Norway
SMIT NEYLAND	2003	Maritime Partners Norway

G.R.T. 7.0 GRT **Dimensions** 12.3m x 2.83m x 0.89m **Speed** 35 knots **Complement** 2

Notes
A class of 12 metre Fast Patrol Craft which operate on Range Safety Duties at Dover, Portland and Pembroke. Have replaced the former RCT Sir and Honours class launches in this role.

79

RAMPED CRAFT LOGISTIC

Vessel	Pennant Number	Completion Date	Builder
ARROMANCHES	L105	1987	James & Stone
ANDALSNES	L107	1984	James & Stone
AKYAB	L109	1984	James & Stone
AACHEN	L110	1986	James & Stone
AREZZO	L111	1986	James & Stone
AUDEMER	L113	1987	James & Stone

Displacement 165 tons **Dimensions** 33m x 8m x 1.5m **Speed** 9 knots
Complement 6.

Notes

Smaller - "all purpose" landing craft capable of carrying up to 96 tons. In service in coastal waters around Cyprus (ANDALSNES and AKYAB) and UK. ARROMANCHES was formerly AGHEILA (re-named 1994 when original vessel was sold). Several vessels sport green and black camouflage scheme.

AIRCRAFT OF THE FLEET AIR ARM

NICK NEWNS

British Aerospace HARRIER

Variants GR7, GR9, GR9A, T12.
Role Short take off, vertical landing (STOVL) strike, ground-attack and reconnaissance aircraft.
Engine 1 x Rolls Royce Pegasus 107 turbofan rated at 23,800lb thrust.
Span 30' 4"   **Length** 47' 1"   **Height** 11' 7"   **Max weight** 31,000lb.
Max speed 575 knots at low level.   **Crew** 1 pilot.
Avionics Hughes Angle Rate Bombing System (ARBS); thermal and infra-red imaging sensors; Zeus defensive aids suite including radar warning, ECM & chaff & flare dispensers; Night Vision Goggle (NVG) compatible cockpit.
Armament Up to 13,000lb of weapons on nine hard points. Inner wing stations can carry up to 2,000lb, outer wing stations intended only for Sidewinder missiles. Weapons include AGM 65 TV and IR guided air to surface missiles (ASM); Brimstone anti-armour ASM; Paveway II & III Laser Guided Bombs (LGB); CRV 7 rocket pods and up to 4 Sidewinder infra-red guided Air to Air Missiles (AAM). Inner wing stations carry 100 or 190 gallon drop tanks. A reconnaissance pod can be carried on the fuselage centre station.
Squadron service 800 squadron from April, 801 squadron from September 2006. The last Sea Harriers are to be withdrawn from service in March 2006 when 801 converts to the GR9. Both RN squadrons are to have a nominal complement of 9 Harriers. The GR9 has the up-rated Pegasus 107 engine, the 9A will in addition have the full weapons capability with open-architecture computer system for targeting and weapons management. 20 (Reserve) squadron RAF will train both RN and RAF pilots using T12 two-seaters in addition to GR9s. The RN squadrons are shore-based at RAF Cottesmore, training is based at RAF Wittering. RNAS Yeovilton ceases to be a fighter base when the last Sea Harriers are withdrawn from service.

European Helicopter Industries EH101 MERLIN

Variants HM1
Role Anti-submarine and Maritime patrol
Engine 3 x Rolls-Royce Turbomeca RTM322 turboshafts each developing 2,100 shp
Length 74' 10" **Width** 14' 10" **Height** 21' 10" **Main Rotor Diameter** 61'
Max Speed 167 kts **Range** 625 nm
Crew 3 (Pilot, Observer and Aircrewman)
Avionics Blue Kestrel 360 degree search radar, Orange Reaper ESM, passive and active sonar systems and AQS903 digital processor.
Armament 4 lightweight torpedoes or depth charges.
Squadron service 700M (OEU), 814, 820, 824 829 Squadrons

Notes

The Merlin HM1 is an advanced anti-submarine helicopter that can also be used for surface surveillance, although, surprisingly, it lacks a weapon capable of attacking surface warships. Trials are being carried out with a Wescam video and infra-red search pod as part of an investigation into a capability upgrade programme for the type. Fast and agile for its size, Merlin is flown by a single pilot. 829 is the parent squadron for 6 flights that operate from Type 23 frigates and an HQ flight. A Merlin of 700M Squadron has been fitted with a Wescam MX15 electro optical device for trials. During trials the system has positively identified vessels visually out to 70nm.

Westland SEA KING

Developed for the Royal Navy from the Sikorsky SH-3D, the basic Sea King airframe is still used in a number of different roles. The following details are common to all:

Engines 2 x 1600shp Rolls Royce Gnome H 1400 – 1 free power turbines.
Rotor Diameter 62' 0" **Length** 54' 9" **Height** 17' 2" **Max Weight** 21,400lb
Max Speed 125 knots.

MARITIME PHOTOGRAPHIC

HAR 5 / 6 and Mk6 (CR)

Roles Utility; COD (Carrier Onboard Delivery); SAR.
Crew 2 pilots, 1 observer and 1 aircrewman.
Avionics Sea Searcher radar; Orange Crop passive ESM equipment.
Armament A 7.62mm machine gun can be mounted in the doorway.
Squadron Service 846 NAS (Mk6 (CR)); 771 NAS all other variants.
Notes The HAR5 continues to provide excellent SAR service in the south west approaches and at Prestwick, where three aircraft are detached from 771 NAS for SAR duties. Some HAS6 airframes, stripped of their radar and sonar, designated Mk6 (CR), are used by Commando squadrons while their HC4s go through a refurbishment programme. Others, parented by 771 NAS at Culdrose, will be embarked in carriers for combat SAR and COD duties. Undercarriage is fixed in the down position in the Mk6 (CR).

ASaC 7

Role Airborne Surveilance and Control. **Crew:** 1 pilot and 2 observers.
Avionics Upgraded Thales Searchwater radar, Orange Crop passive ESM, Enhanced Communications System, Joint Tactical Information Distribution System (Link 16)
Squadron Service 849 HQ, 849A and 849B Flights in commission.
Notes Used for the Airborne Surveillance and Control (ASaC) of the airspace over a

maritime force. Can also be used for surface search utilising their sophisticated, computerised long range radar. 849HQ acts as a training and trials unit at Culdrose. There were 13 conversions of airframes to this role, with a further two authorised in 2004 to replace aircraft lost in Operation Telic in the Gulf.

• NICK NEWNS

HC 4

Role Commando assault and utility transport.
Crew 2 pilots and 1 aircrewman.
Armament Door mounted 7.62mm machine gun.
Squadron Service 845, 846 and 848 Squadrons.
Notes The HC4 has a fixed undercarriage with no sponsons or radome. It is equipped to carry up to 17 troops in the cabin or underslung loads of up to 6000 lbs. The three Commando Support squadrons are based at Yeovilton but (together with 847 NAS with its Army-type Lynx aircaft) form part of the Joint Helicopter Command (JHC) based at Wilton, a tri-Service formation whose purpose is to maximise the effectiveness of all battlefield helicopters. The Commando Support squadrons train to operate in all environments, from arctic to tropical, and can embark or detach at short notice to support 3 Commando Brigade or as required by the JHC. The HC4 has extensive armour plating and a sophisticated defensive aids suite.

• NICK NEWNS **Sea King ASaC7 hovers with a Lynx HAS3 in the foreground**

Westland LYNX

Variants HAS 3, HMA 8, AH 7.
Roles Surface search and attack; anti-submarine attack; SAR; troop carrying.
Engines 2 x 900hp Rolls Royce GEM BS 360-07-26 free shaft turbines.
Rotor diameter 42' 0" **Length** 39' 1" **Height** 11' 0" **Max Weight** 9,500lb.
Max Speed 150 knots. **Crew** 1 pilot and 1 observer.
Avionics SEA SPRAY radar. Orange Crop passive ESM equipment. Sea Owl Passive
Infrared Device (Mk 8).
Armament External pylons carry up to 4 - SEA SKUA air to surface missiles or 2 x
STINGRAY torpedoes, depth charges and markers. 1 door mounted M3M 0.5" machine
gun. Standard configuration for board and search operations now 1 x door mounted
M3M, 1 x pylon mounted Sea Skua and rope for "rapid-roping" deployment of troops.
Squadron Service 702, 815 and 847 squadrons in commission.

Notes Lynx OEU (Operational Evaluation Unit) develops operational tactics for HMA 8
aircraft. 702 NAS is the training squadron. 815 squadron is the parent unit for single aircraft ships flights. Both squadrons are based at Yeovilton. Ships' Flights are divided
approximately equally between HAS 3 and HMA 8 aircraft. Another version of the Lynx,
the AH7, is operated by 847 NAS in a Commando Support role. There are 35 airframes
each of the HMA8 and HAS3 versions. Current out of service date for the Lynx is 2015.

TAILORED AIR GROUPS

ILLUSTRIOUS, ARK ROYAL and OCEAN no longer have dedicated air groups which embark every time the ship is at sea. Instead they embark Tailored Air Groups (TAG) chosen to fulfil the specific mission for which the ships are to be deployed. In the first two ships up to three types can be embarked concurrently, selected from Harrier, Merlin, Sea King, Chinook and Apache squadrons. The Sea Kings can be HC 4 utility versions or the ASaC 7s operated by 849 Squadron. OCEAN cannot support fixed-wing aircraft operationally although they can launch and recover from her deck. From 2006 TAGs will embark with appropriate force commanders, responsible to PJHQ Northwood for the tactical employment of their air assets and to their own Joint Force HQ for their operational readiness. Typically, a strike TAG would have an RN captain or RAF group captain as force commander. A battlefield helicopter TAG could have an Army colonel as force commander. This new operational structure introduces the force concepts that the MoD expects to employ in the future carrier in the next decade. It is a doctrine unique to the UK and not being considered by any other maritime nation.

• NICK NEWNS

Westland APACHE AH1

Variants AH 1
Role Attack and reconnaissance helicopter.
Engines 2 x Rolls Royce/Turbomeca RTM 322 turboshafts.
Rotor Diameter 17' 2" **Length** 58' 3" **Height** 15' 3" **Max Weight** 15,075lb.
Max Speed 150 knots **Crew:** 2 pilots
Avionics Helicopter integrated defensive Aids Suite (HIDAS); Longbow radar, optical and infra-red target acquisition sensors.
Armament Up to 16 AGM 114 Hellfire anti-tank guided weapons; up to 4 Sidewinder air-to-air missiles; M230 30mm cannon with 1,160 rounds (chain gun); up to 76 CRV 7 unguided rockets.

Squadron Service 656 Squadron, 9 Regiment AAC allocated for maritime tasking.
Notes Army Air Corps Apaches have been cleared for embarked operations from ILLUSTRIOUS, ARK ROYAL and OCEAN. With other joint assets they can form part of Tailored Air Groups (TAG) embarked for specific operational and training missions.

• NICK NEWNS

Boeing CHINOOK HC2

Variants HC 2
Role Battlefield transport helicopter.
Engines 2 x 3,750 shp Avco Lycoming T55-L-712 turboshafts.
Rotor Diameter 60' 0" **Length** 98' 9" **Height** 18' 8" **Max Weight** 50,000lb
Max Speed 160 knots **Crew** 2 pilots, 1 aircrewman.
Avionics Infra-red jammer; chaff & flare dispenser, missile warning system.
Armament Up to 2 x M 134 miniguns and 1 x M 60 machine gun.
Squadron Service 18 Squadron RAF is declared in the maritime role.
Notes RAF Chinook squadrons form part of the Joint Helicopter Force with the RN commando squadrons. 18 Squadron aircraft embarked in ARK ROYAL during Operation Telic in 2003 and are frequently used to provide heavy lift during amphibious expeditionary operations. They are too large to strike down into the hangars in OCEAN, ILLUSTRIOUS and ARK ROYAL and have to have their rotor blades manually removed for parking on deck as they lack a conventional blade fold mechanism. The new CVF is being designed with Chinook operations in mind.

FLEET TARGET GROUP

792 Naval Air Squadron was commissioned at RNAS Culdrose in November 2001, from the Fleet Target Group which had transferred its operations from RNAS Portland on its closure in 1998.

The Squadron operates Mirach 100/5 unmanned high subsonic drones used to test the Sea Dart Missile System fitted to Type 42 Destroyers. They are also used to test Sidewinder missiles on Harriers and RAF Tornados. Meteor SPA of Italy builds the MIRACH 100/5 and 37 were ordered for 792 NAS. Take off is assisted by two rockets that fall away once the drone is airborne. The drone can be controlled by a ship or shore based operator.

The Italian company, Galileo Avionica, supplies the MIRACH 100/5 naval variant to the UK. In 2003 it signed a major contract with QinetiQ, the UK company responsible for British firing range operations. In this case, the MIRACH 100/5 was selected under the Replacement Aerial Target System (RATS) program to replace the British Jindivik aerial target previously used at the Aberporth range.

The MIRACH 100/5 can be launched from the flight deck of a Type 42, Fort or Rover Class RFAs, and is also launched from a land based site operated by QinetiQ at Aberporth in Wales. Once the MIRACH has completed its mission, it parachutes down into the sea to be recovered by Lynx Helicopter and used again. An RAF Nimrod is always present while the drone is flying to ensure the range is clear at all times.

OTHER AIRCRAFT TYPES IN ROYAL NAVY SERVICE DURING 2006

British Aerospace HAWK

Engine 1 x Adour Mk 151 5200 lbs thrust.
Crew 1 or 2 Pilots (both service and civilian)
Notes Used by Fleet Requirements and Aircraft Direction Unit (FRADU) at Culdrose to provide support for training of RN ships, RN Flying Standards Flight and as airborne targets for the Aircraft Direction School. The aircraft are operated by Babcock.

British Aerospace JETSTREAM T2 and T3

Engines 2 x 940hp Turbomeca ASTAZOU 16D turboprops. (T3 Garrett turboprops).
Crew 1 or 2 pilots, 2 student observers plus 3 other seats.
Notes T2's are used by 750 Squadron at Culdrose for training Fleet Air Arm Observers. T3's are used by the 750 Heron detachment at Yeovilton for operational support/communications flying.

• LEE HOWARD

Aerospatiale AS365N DAUPHIN 2

Engines 2 x Turbomeca Arriel 1C1.
Crew 1 or 2 pilots.
Notes Operated by British International from Plymouth City Airport under MoD COMR (Civil Owned Military Registered) contract. Used to transfer Sea Training staff from shore and between ships operating in the Plymouth sea training areas during work-ups. Aircraft are also used for Guided Weapons System Calibration and Naval Gunfire Support.

• LEE HOWARD

GROB G115 D-2

Used for the flying grading of new entry aircrew and the initial conversion of Rotary to Fixed Wing pilots. They are owned and operated by a division of Short Brothers plc and operate from Plymouth City Airport on behalf of 727 NAS.

Royal Navy Historic Flight

The RNHF is supported financially by the Swordfish Heritage Trust. The Historic Flight has been civilianised since 1993. The current (2006) holding of aircraft is:

Flying: 1 Sea Hawk, 1 Sea Fury.
Under Repair: 3 Fairey Swordfish.

• NICK NEWNS   **Royal Navy Historic Flight Sea Fury**

• NICK NEWNS   **Royal Navy Historic Flight Seahawk**

WEAPONS OF THE ROYAL NAVY

Sea Launched Missiles

◀ Trident II D5

The American built Lockheed Martin Trident 2 (D5) submarine launched strategic missiles are Britain's only nuclear weapons and form the UK contribution to the NATO strategic deterrent. 16 missiles, each capable of carrying up to 6 UK manufactured thermonuclear warheads (but currently limited to 4 under current government policy), are aboard each of the Vanguard class SSBNs. Trident has a maximum range of 12,000 km and is powered by a three stage rocket motor. Launch weight is 60 tonnes, overall length and width are 13.4 metres and 2.1 metres respectively.

Tomahawk (BGM-109)

This is a land attack cruise missile with a range of 1600 km and can be launched from a variety of platforms including surface ships and submarines. Some 65 of the latter version were purchased from America to arm Trafalgar class SSNs with the first being delivered to the Royal Navy for trials during 1998. Tomahawk is fired in a disposal container from the submarine's conventional torpedo tubes and is then accelerated to its subsonic cruising speed by a booster rocket motor before a lightweight F-107 turbojet takes over for the cruise. Its extremely accurate guidance system means that small targets can be hit with precision at maximum range, as was dramatically illustrated in the Gulf War and Afghanistan. Total weight of the submarine version, including its launch capsule is 1816 kg, it carries a 450 kg warhead, length is 6.4 metres and wingspan (fully extended) 2.54 m. Fitted in T class submarines.

Harpoon

The Harpoon is a sophisticated anti-ship missile using a combination of inertial guidance and active radar homing to attack targets out to a range of 130 km, cruising at Mach 0.9 and carrying a 227 kg warhead. Fitted to the Batch II Type 22 and Type 23 frigates. It is powered by a lightweight turbojet but is accelerated at launch by a booster rocket. The RN also deploys the UGM-84 submarine launched version aboard its Swiftsure and Trafalgar class SSNs.

Sea Dart

A medium range area defence anti aircraft missile powered by a ramjet and solid fuel booster rocket. Maximum effective range is in the order of 80 km and the missile accelerates to a speed of Mach 3.5. It forms the main armament of the Type 42 destroyers. Missile weight 550 kg, length 4.4 m, wingspan 0.91 m.

Sea Wolf

Short range rapid reaction anti-missile missile and anti-aircraft weapon. The complete weapon system, including radars and fire control computers, is entirely automatic in operation. Type 22 frigates carry two sextuple Sea Wolf launchers but the subsequent Type 23 frigates carry 32 Vertical Launch Seawolf (VLS) in a silo on the foredeck. Basic missile data: weight 82 kg, length 1.9 m, wingspan 56 cm, range c.56 km, warhead 13.4 kg. The VLS missile is basically similar but has jettisonable tandem boost rocket motors.

Air Launched Missiles

Sea Skua

A small anti ship missile developed by British Aerospace arming the Lynx helicopters carried by various frigates and destroyers. The missile weighs 147 kg, has a length of 2.85 m and a span of 62 cm. Powered by solid fuel booster and sustainer rocket motors, it has a range of over 15 km at high subsonic speed. Sea Skua is particularly effective against patrol vessels and fast attack craft, as was demonstrated in both the Falklands and Gulf Wars.

Sidewinder

This is one of the world's most successful short range air to air missiles. The latest AIM-9L version carried by Harriers uses a heat seeking infra red guidance system and has a range of 18 km. Powered by a solid fuel rocket motor boosting it to speeds of Mach 2.5, it weighs 86.6 kg and is 2.87 m long

AMRAAM

The Hughes AIM-120 Advanced Medium Range Air To Air Missile arms the Sea Harrier FA.2 and has a range of around 50 km. Weight 157 kg, length 3.65 m. Coupled with the Blue Vixen multi mode radar, the AMRAAM gives a substantial boost to the aircraft's capability as an air defence interceptor, allowing Beyond Visual Range (BVR) engagements.

Guns

114mm Vickers Mk8

The Royal Navy's standard medium calibre general purpose gun which arms the later Type 22s, Type 23 frigates and Type 42 destroyers. A new electrically operated version, the Mod 1, recognised by its angular turret, was introduced in 2001 and will be fitted in the Type 23, Type 22, some Type 42 and the Type 45 classes. Rate of fire: 25 rounds/min. Range: 22,000 m. Weight of Shell: 21 kg.

Goalkeeper

A highly effective automatic Close in Weapons System (CIWS) designed to shoot down missiles and aircraft which have evaded the outer layers of a ships defences. The complete system, designed and built in Holland, is on an autonomous mounting and includes radars, fire control computers and a 7-barrel 30 mm Gatling gun firing 4200 rounds/min. Goalkeeper is designed to engage targets between 350 and 1500 metres away.

Phalanx

A US built CIWS designed around the Vulcan 20 mm rotary cannon. Rate of fire is 3000 rounds/min and effective range is c.1500 m. Fitted in Type 42 destroyers, ARK ROYAL, OCEAN and the FORT VICTORIA class.

DS30B 30mm

Single 30mm mounting carrying an Oerlikon 30mm gun. Fitted to Type 23 frigates and various patrol vessels and MCMVs. In August 2005 it was announced that the DS30B fitted in Type 23 frigates was to be upgraded to DS30M Mk 2 to include new direct-drive digital servos and the replacement of the earlier Oerlikon KCB cannon with the ATK Mk 44 Bushmaster II 30 mm gun. Consideration is already being given to purchasing additional DS30M Mk 2 systems for minor war vessels and auxiliaries.

GAM BO 20mm

A simple hand operated mounting carrying a single Oerlikon KAA 200 automatic cannon firing 1000 rounds/min. Maximum range is 2000 m. Carried by most of the fleet's major warships except the Type 23 frigates.

20mm Mk.7A

The design of this simple but reliable weapon dates back to World War II but it still provides a useful increase in firepower, particularly for auxiliary vessels and RFAs. Rate of fire 500-800 rounds/min.

Close Range Weapons

In addition to the major weapons systems, all RN ships carry a variety of smaller calibre weapons to provide protection against emerging terrorist threats in port and on the high seas such as small fast suicide craft. In addition it is sometimes preferable, during policing or stop and search operations to have a smaller calibre weapon available. Depending upon the operational environment ships may be seen armed with varying numbers of pedestal mounted General Purpose Machine Guns (GPMG). Another addition to the close in weapons is the Mk 44 Mini Gun a total of 150 of which have been procured from the United States as a fleetwide fit. Fitted to a naval post mount, the Minigun is able to fire up to 3,000 rounds per minute, and is fully self-contained (operating off battery power).

Torpedoes

Stingray

A lightweight anti submarine torpedo which can be launched from ships, helicopters or aircraft. In effect it is an undersea guided missile with a range of 11 km at 45 knots or 7.5 km at 60 knots. Length 2.1 m, diameter 330 mm. Aboard Type 42s and Type 22s Stingray is fired from triple tubes forming part of the Ships Torpedo Weapon System (STWS) but the newer Type 23s have the Magazine Torpedo Launch System (MTLS) with internal launch tubes. Sting Ray Mod 1 (which is to enter service in 2006) is intended to prosecute the same threats as the original Sting Ray but with an enhanced capability against small conventionally powered submarines and an improved shallow-water performance.

Spearfish

Spearfish is a submarine-launched heavyweight torpedo which has replaced Tigerfish. Claimed by the manufacturers to be the world's fastest torpedo, capable of over 70 kts, its sophisticated guidance system includes an onboard acoustic processing suite and tactical computer backed up by a command and control wire link to the parent submarine. Over 20ft in length and weighing nearly two tons, Spearfish is fired from the standard 21-inch submarine torpedo tube and utilises an advanced bi-propellant gas turbine engine for higher performance.

At the end of the line ...

Readers may well find other warships afloat which are not mentioned in this book. The majority have fulfilled a long and useful life and are now relegated to non-seagoing duties. The following list gives details of their current duties:

Pennant No	Ship	Remarks
	BRITANNIA	Ex Royal Yacht at Leith. Open to the public.
	CAROLINE	RNR Drill Ship at Belfast, Northern Ireland.
A134	RAME HEAD	Escort Maintenance Vessel – Royal Marines Training Ship in Fareham Creek (Portsmouth)
C35	BELFAST	World War II Cruiser Museum ship – Pool of London. Open to the public daily . Tel: 020 7940 6300
D23	BRISTOL	Type 82 Destroyer – Sea Cadet Training Ship at Portsmouth.
D73 S17	CAVALIER OCELOT	World War II Destroyer & Oberon class Submarine Museum Ships at Chatham. Partially open to the public. Tel: 01634 823800
F126 S21 M1115	PLYMOUTH ONYX BRONINGTON	Type 12 Frigate, Oberon class Submarine & Ton class Minesweeper. Museum Ships at Birkenhead, Wirral. Open to the public daily. Tel: 0151 650 1573
S67	ALLIANCE	Submarine – Museum Ship at Gosport Open to the public daily. Tel: 023 92 511349
M1151 M1154	IVESTON KELLINGTON	(Thurrock) } Static Sea Cadet (Stockton upon Tees) } Training Vessels

At the time of publishing (December 2005) the following ships were laid up in long term storage or awaiting sale.

PORTSMOUTH: Intrepid; Fearless; Newcastle; Glasgow; Cardiff; Bridport; Sandown; Inverness; Brecon; Cottesmore; Dulverton: Leeds Castle.

PLYMOUTH: Splendid, Courageous; Conqueror; Valiant; Warspite.

ROSYTH: Resolution; Renown; Repulse; Revenge; Swiftsure; Dreadnought; Churchill.